HOW TO LIVE

HOW TO LIVE

Helen Rickerby

AUCKLAND UNIVERSITY PRESS

*For N
(who would be A,
if not for A)*

Contents

Notes on the unsilent woman	1
The now and the maybe	13
A pillow book	15
Ban Zhao	17
Rocks	25
Mr Andersen, you heartbreaker you	26
I knew we were really supposed to take the audio guides	27
How to die	29
George Eliot: a life	31
Navigating by the stars	57
The happiness of Mary Shelley	60
How to live through this	64
Forks	65
Four stories about kindness	66
How to live	69
Notes	85
Acknowledgements	87

Notes on the unsilent woman
Hipparchia of Maroneia c. 350–c. 280 BC

1.   Hipparchia: hip-park-ee-ah (and Crates: krah-tease).

2.   Perhaps the first thing you need to know is that women in ancient Athens didn't get out much. No dinner parties, no debate, no public life. Unless you were already ruined. Or unless you were Hipparchia.

3.   'When it comes to silencing women, Western culture has had thousands of years of practise.' Mary Beard, *Women and Power*. What is a woman? What is culture? What is silence?

4.   Silence isn't always not speaking. Silence is sometimes an erasure. We don't know much about her, but we know she spoke. Sometimes, like today, I don't want to leave the house. I don't want to speak. I don't want to write. I don't feel like saying anything – so much, too much, has already been said. We all know what someone who speaks looks like, someone who should be taken seriously.

5.   But I do have something to say. I want to say that she lived. I want to say that she lived, and she spoke and she was not silent.

6.   It seems to me that poetry usually begins with the self and works its way outwards; and the essay, perhaps, starts outwards and works its way in towards the self.

7.   They were both rich kids who gave it away. Him before he met her, she for him – though I suspect it was really for philosophy: love of wisdom. He left everything back in Thebes, to his sons, to the poor, or he threw it all into the sea, depending on the version.

8.   I found her when I went looking for the philosophers who were also women. Where were they? You find them as soon as you look. Perhaps not many – few had the opportunity, the education, the space, and of the few, fewer are remembered. History has that way of erasing women – women are so forgettable – and of the few who are remembered, many are called something else: prophetess, wise woman, mystic, witch. Writer. We all know what a philosopher looks like: he has a beard, a robe, and carries a staff. We all know what a philosopher looks like: he has a serious look and two-day stubble above his turtleneck sweater.

9.   I am constantly astonished at the number of exceptional women there have been. Enheduanna. Mary Wollstonecraft. Christine de Pisan. Jael. Murasaki Shikibu. Hypatia. Te Aokapurangi. Mary Shelley. Boudica. Sacagawea. Pope Joan. Joan of Arc. Jane Austen. Sosipatra. Harriet Martineau.

10.   What might look like waiting is often watching. Sometimes I think I am dead, but that's what lying fallow looks like. At first. Before the weeds grow.

11.   There was already one philosopher in her family. Metrocles (meh-trock-klees), first born, first son, had claimed the title first. There was no two-day stubble above

his turtleneck toga – that sort of thing wouldn't go down well at the Academy, where he hung with the popular kids. That's why the whole family picked up sticks from Maroneia, schlepping south for the sake of higher learning. But, one day, while rehearsing a speech, Metrocles farted. They say you never die of shame, but he was so embarrassed that it seemed like a good option. He locked himself in his room and refused to eat. Someone thought to fetch Crates, the most famous philosopher in Athens. Crates wandered on over, made himself at home and started cooking a bean stew. 'What you gotta understand, M', he said, 'is that it's perfectly natural', and then farted himself. Once they've laughed, they're halfway saved. And so that's probably how she met him, as he mooched around her brother's room, saving his life. Perhaps she was grateful. Perhaps that was how she fell.

12. Perhaps I should ban 'perhaps'. It is a shrinking word. An ensmallening word, when I feel that it is probably my feminist duty to use big, bold words. To be definite. 'Probably' is probably another of those words.

13. Silence can be the worst weapon. What's wrong? Nothing.

14. My childhood experiences of beans tended towards the negative. The hairy, stringy runner beans my parents grew on the tall wire fence at the far end of the vegetable garden, just before the ground fell away to a bush-filled abyss. The grey rubbery broad beans, of which, in an attempt to broaden our tastes, we had to eat at least one. I can feel again that slightly choking sensation as I swallowed it

whole to avoid its flavour. Perhaps Pythagoras had some similar formative experiences that prompted him to take against beans in a serious way. Perhaps they upset his stomach. Perhaps he opposed flatulence. Perhaps they reminded him too much of the souls of his ancestors. Beans may have been an ancient symbol of death, but Crates didn't care. He was a cynic philosopher.

15. 'It saddens me, and tends to make me silent, when men strongly believe that argument is a battle in which one person wins and the other loses.' Cecile T. Tougas, *Presenting Women Philosophers.*

16. Why are the words of a woman so terrifying?

17. 'But Crates with only his wallet and tattered cloak laughed out his life jocosely, as if he had been always at a festival.' Plutarch, *Moralia*. I imagine Crates as a bit like my friend B. B likes to take credit for other people's relationships and talks about how he got them together, or how he helped them sort it out when they broke up that time. Some of this is true. Crates would wander into other people's houses during times of discord, which often coincided with dinner time. And by the time he left, rifts would have been healed, wives talking again to husbands, fathers to sons, brother to brother, brother to sister.

18. Laura Bassi. Maria Gaetana Agnesi. Catherine of Siena. Queen Victoria. Queen Christina. Héloïse. Sappho. Aphra Behn. Emmeline Pankhurst. Margaret of Anjou. Damaris Cudworth Masham. Triệu Thị Trinh. Harriet Taylor Mill.

19. Silence might not be not speaking. It might be listening. It can be hard to tell the difference.

20. 'Even fools are thought wise if they keep silent, and discerning if they hold their tongues.' Proverbs 17:28.

21. I must apologise – we're so far in, and she is not even yet the protagonist in her own story. Hold on, let me fix that.

22. Hipparchia did the choosing. The other boys bored her, though she could have had her pick. Crates, she decided, was the man for her. Despite his age (older). Despite his clothes (manky). Despite his likely lack of personal hygiene. Her parents tried to change her mind, but – melodrama running in the family – she said if she couldn't marry him, she would kill herself. Crates, keen to avoid familial discord, said he'd try to dissuade her: he stood before her, put down his staff, took off his cloak. Naked, he said, 'Here is your bridegroom, here are his possessions.' Choose him, choose his life. 'I'm in!' she said. She had been waiting for an excuse to slough off her chiton, snuggle into her own man's cloak, swap her house for the streets. 'So long, Expected Life, I can't say I'll be missing you.'

23. I have no truck with the decluttering fad – it seems to me to be another way to make women feel guilty – but when I returned to my house after several weeks of living out of a carry-on suitcase, I found I had a yearning to rid myself of my many possessions. *Oh heavy burdens!*

24. A conversation requires both voice and silence. Listening and speaking. Listening to the voice, and listening to the silence. Speaking and being heard. Listening and hearing.

25. A monologue is a simpler thing.

26. What we have left of what Hipparchia wrote:
[

                                                                ]

27. I love the way thought will leap across a space, across a silence. We sometimes won't even perceive a gap. Sometimes we will fill it.

28. George Eliot. Eleanor of Aquitaine. Judith. Anne Conway. Marie Curie. Sofonisba Anguissola. Artemisia Gentileschi. Wu Zetian. The Queen of Sheba. Catherine the

Great. Hinematioro. Harriet Beecher Stowe. Helen Keller. Hildegard von Bingen. Diotima.

29. 'If a woman speaks out of turn her teeth will be smashed with a burnt brick.' Sumerian law, *c.* 2400 BC.

30. Cynic simply meant dog-like. Diogenes 'the dog' lived happily in a wine jar. Cynosure: the pole star, the guiding light.

31. They lived as equals. The whole city was their playground and they romped like young pups, like wild dogs. They slept between the columns, fucked in the open air: if it's good enough for private, it's good enough for public. They were anaideia, shameless, without shame.

32. Every year, H told me, she chooses a motto, a theme: just one word. I have forgotten all the rest, but one year it was 'Shameless'. Shameless hussy. You should be ashamed of yourself. What a shame.

33. '[A] woman should as modestly guard against exposing her voice to outsiders as she would guard against stripping off her clothes.' Plutarch, *Moralia*.

34. Barbara Bodichon. Kate Sheppard. Meri Te Tai Mangakāhia. Sophie Scholl. Nur Jahan. Nefertiti. Queen Elizabeth I. Ban Zhao. Empress Matilda. Margaret Cavendish. Elena Cornaro Piscopia. Phillis Wheatley. Hatshepsut.

35. But. I am a believer in silence. The value of silence. The power of silence. The space that isn't an absence but

a presence. A pause that is bigger than the noise that surrounds it. A gap that is a mirror. A gulf that is a bridge. The emptiness that is rejuvenating. The space that is full of more than it could ever contain.

36. Maybe my favourite part of this story is when Hipparchia went with Crates to a dinner party. There she meets her nemesis: Theodorus the atheist. 'Who is the woman who has left behind the shuttles of the loom?' he asked, affronted. Anti-Penelope. Unnatural monster. She replied, 'I, Theodorus, am that person. Does it seem wrong to you that I devote my time to philosophy rather than the loom?' And maybe that same night, or perhaps another, she said, 'Whatever you do cannot be said to be wrong, and so if I do it, it can't be wrong either. For example, if you hit yourself, it wouldn't be wrong, so if I hit you, it wouldn't be wrong either.' I guess he lacked a decent comeback: he grabbed her cloak and tried to pull it off. Exposing her body. She stood her ground. Shameless. I see her triumphant, one woman in a room of men.

37. 'Hipparchia is a genus of butterflies within the family Nymphalidae.' 'Hipparchia (genus)', *Wikipedia*.

38. Women who speak have always been monstrous. That twisty sphinx, those tempting sirens; better plug your ears with wax, boys.

39. 'I'm sick of "liberal" men whose mask slips every time a woman displeases them, who reach immediately for crude and humiliating words associated with femaleness, act like old-school misogynists and then preen themselves

as though they've been brave. When you do this, Mr Liberal Cool Guy, you ally yourself, wittingly or not, with the men who send women violent pornographic images and rape threats, who try by every means possible to intimidate women out of politics and public spaces, both real and digital. "Cunt", "whore" and, naturally, rape. We're too ugly to rape, or we need raping, or we need raping and killing. Every woman I know who has dared express an opinion publicly has endured this kind of abuse at least once, rooted in an apparent determination to humiliate or intimidate her on the basis that she is female.' J. K. Rowling, Twitter, 9 June 2017.

40. But probably she didn't feel so triumphant – one woman in a room of men. Maybe she feared. For her life. Maybe she went home – wherever that was – and cried. Maybe Crates said, 'Don't worry, things like that happen to me all the time.' But they didn't.

41. 'Why should she live, to fill the world with words?' William Shakespeare, *Henry VI Pt 3*.

42. Some things we tell because we don't want them to have power over us. Some things we never tell because we don't want them to have power over us.

43. There are things we didn't think we could tell.

44. There are things we didn't think we needed to tell. 'Why didn't you tell anyone?' Let's pretend that everyone didn't already know.

45. I didn't want that to be what you think of when you look at me.

46. Embarrassed is another of those ensmallening words. *You're* the one who should be embarrassed.

47. 'Let the woman learn in silence with all subjection. But I suffer not a woman to teach, nor to usurp authority over the man, but to be in silence. For Adam was first formed, then Eve.' St Paul, 1 Timothy 2:11–13.

48. P and I are talking about Mary Beard. 'Are we allowed to like her?' P asks. 'Didn't she write that thing?' I say I don't know, I haven't read much by her, but what I've read I've liked. But we're thinking of Germaine Greer, of Lena Dunham, of even Margaret Atwood, who said that thing that time. If you can't say anything nice, then don't say anything at all. Be seen and not heard. I would rather people just said nice things. I like women to be nice. I like men to be nice too. But I assume women will be nicer.

49. I would like to be able to say that it was the patriarchy that stopped me talking on social media, but it wasn't, not directly.

50. Since I began writing this poem, women have begun to speak. No. Women have begun to be heard. I don't understand what happened, but suddenly things that we all knew – all women at least – became big news. Suddenly women's words had the power to take down a Hollywood mogul, and who will be next? Suddenly the Law Society

is shocked. 'Why didn't you say anything before?' Why weren't you listening?

51. We all know what a prime minister looks like: he is a white man with a dark suit. Sometimes the speed of change astounds me.

52. C tells me he's the third most talkative (i.e. dominating) person in his book club. First and second are both also men. Number one is aware of his tendency to dominate, and so makes an effort to hand on the conversation; but he usually hands it on to another man. C says this is very typical behaviour; he wrote something about it as a psych honours student. B says that, having once been made aware of this, he now always tries to hand the conversation over to a woman. That's very admirable, I think, though I cannot remember many instances of him handing over a conversation to anyone at all.

53. Hipparchia wrote treatises such as *Philosophical Hypotheses*, *Epichiremas* and *Questions to Theodorus*. Letters, jokes, philosophical refutations. All are lost. (Crates wrote *Knapsack* and *Praise of the Lentil*.)

54. L is talking about how she always felt she needed to be small, to shrink down, not take up any space, but now when dealing with him, the man who is trying to make her feel small, she imagines herself expanding, filling up the room like a gas.

55. Manuela Sáenz. Mary Astell. Anna Maria von Schurman. Margaret Fuller. Nzinga. Tomoe Gozen. Kimpa

Vita. Cleopatra. Anna Julia Cooper. Hortensia. Sojourner Truth. Charlotte Perkins Gilman. Zenobia. How many does it take before they are no longer exceptional?

56. H tells us she is writing long poems now as a feminist act. No more I'm sorry for taking up space. No more tiny apologetic little pieces of embroidery. No more thank you for the small scrap of attention. No more whispering.

57. 'In the greatest art, one is always aware of the things that cannot be said . . . of the contradiction between expression and the presence of the inexpressible – stylistic devices are also techniques of avoidance. The most potent elements in a work of art are, often, its silences.' Susan Sontag, 'On Style'.

58. Oh, but I still wish I knew what you said, Lady Butterfly. I wish I could hear your words.

The now and the maybe

i

Every time you step across the threshold it's the same. You're stepping into more than just a house. You're seeing not just what's here, but what could be – a palimpsest of the now and the maybe. You consider where the couch will go, the TV, the table; where he will sit, where you will sit, in the evenings, on weekend mornings; whether your middays will be sunny, your afternoons. What about your bookcases? Will they fit? Will you be able to display the books you want to show off, and will there be room in the second bedroom to stow the ones you'd rather hide? *Is* there a second bedroom? Do you need one? Will you have children here? Will you be happy here? Who will you *be* here?

ii

All going well, by now you resent the other people who are trudging through what you already consider to be *your* home. You and he have exchanged wide eyes, whispers, small high noises in the backs of your throats. You have seen your future, and these people are barging through it, through your possible life, who you will be here, how you will live here, the happiness you will have here. You refuse to believe it cannot simply be so, that you need permission; that you need to tender to the gods of housing; that you can be denied this life with no recourse to the appeal court of lost homes, lost futures.

iii

Or, it might be that you're seeing visions of a different kind of future. The sun never makes it through these windows. Despite the new paint, you know it will be damp; all winter you will try to beat the mould, but you will lose. In this room, you will never settle, you will never rest easy. It will be dark all day, you will want to go out, but you lack the energy. You and he will fight. The cupboards will be crammed, you will have to give away too many of your books. Your friends won't admit it to you, but you will know they avoid visiting.

iv

From one alternative future to the other; you drive to three or even more each Sunday. And in every house you leave a little piece of yourself, a little clipping, that stays there, takes root, grows out its days in that future, those futures that could have been yours. Part of you is still sitting, reading a book on the window seat in the lounge of the first house you ever put an offer on; the first one you ever lost.

v

When I walked into this house I felt like I'd stepped into heaven; heaven on the top of a cliff looking out over the city and the harbour, and beyond to the mountains. Heaven at the height of birds' flight, almost cloud height. The life I would live here would clearly involve calmness and considerable amounts of time staring at the sea. 'I want it', I whispered to him, meaning not simply 'I want to buy this house', but, 'I want to be calm and happy. I want to be light and airy. I want to be the clear-headed self, the ideal self that I feel certain I will be here. I want this house to make my future perfect.'

A pillow book

'In life there are two things which are dependable. The pleasures of the
flesh and the pleasures of literature.'
– Sei Shōnagon, *The Pillow Book*

You don't have to be silent
but I am telling you a story

always

I choose what to put on
what to take off

what
and who

Things that have lost their power:
  the first cup of coffee
  the judgement of a stranger
  a lover you no longer love
  the fear of being alone
  the worst thing, when it has already happened

When that philosopher said life must be lived forwards
but can only be understood backwards
he was not thinking of me
  I have lived all kinds of lives

been all kinds of people
girl and boy, old and young
backwards, forwards, sideways

      Skin is a delicate thing

      paper stretches

Tell me new stories
tell me your stories over again

Things that arouse fond memories of the past:
      glitter in the carpet
      the crust of ice on a frosted puddle
      a crushed ticket from a gallery in Venice
      the smoothness of the pages on your fingertips, your lips
      the smell of jasmine

Ban Zhao
(45–c. 116 AD)

Wood / spring

The wind itself is silent
It's only when it hits something
that it makes a sound
I was sure I heard a rushing waterfall
but when I looked, it was only a zephyr in the trees
The wind does not even know it is moving
until it meets an obstacle

If you stay in the same place
you are always moving backwards

*

'I, the unworthy writer, am unsophisticated, unenlightened, and by nature unintelligent, but I am fortunate both to have received not a little favour from my scholarly father, and to have had a cultured mother and instructresses upon whom to rely for a literary education as well as training in good manners.'

*

There are advantages to widowhood, to being left behind. Men will only let women do 'their' work when there is no one else left. And she was the last one: her husband dead; her father, the venerable historian, dead; her brother, his successor, executed (he'd picked the wrong crowd, the losing side). And so it fell to her. She was summoned to court. She got her chance. She finished it: the history of the dynasty, the story of the Han.

*

I Googled: 'What was life like during the Han Dynasty?'
Sometimes I am surprised by how little things have changed
Sometimes by how much

*

Paper is a new sound
She has been made court librarian
and sets the scribes copying from silk
to paper scrolls
From whisper
to rustle

Fire / summer

She was young and green, age fourteen
fearing disgracing more than disgrace

She was the kind of girl who is called
headstrong, those traits
that in a boy might be called determination
She did not know yet that mothers-in-law are always right
even when they are wrong
Especially when they're wrong

*

'If a husband be unworthy, then he possesses nothing by which to control his wife. If a wife be unworthy, then she possesses nothing with which to serve her husband.'

If a man is unworthy, his wife cannot yield.

*

> **yang** (jæŋ) Also Yang. [Chinese *yáng* yang, sun, positive, male genitals.]
>
> In Chinese philosophy, the masculine or positive principle (characterized by light, warmth, dryness, activity, etc.) of the two opposing cosmic forces into which creative energy divides and whose fusion in physical matter brings the phenomenal world into being. Also attrib. or as adj. Cf. yin.

*

Palimpsest is a word I have to look up every time
A palimpsest is a parchment from which the words
have been scraped off so it could be used again
but the old words still show through

Earth / late summer

This is the place of intersection
your life
my life
my time
and the little I know about yours
the little I know about mine
the little I know

*

The join is the weakest part

*

'The correct relationship between a husband and wife is based upon harmony and intimacy, and conjugal love is grounded in proper union. Should actual blows be dealt, how could a matrimonial relationship be preserved?'

*

yin-yang, the combination or fusion of the two cosmic forces; freq. attrib., esp. as yin-yang symbol, a circle divided by an S-shaped line into a dark and a light segment, representing respectively yin and yang, each containing a 'seed' of the other.

*

Men hate women more than they realise
Women hate men less than they deserve

*

'Affairs may be either crooked or straight, words may be either right or wrong.'

*

Is it too much to think of her
lying on her bed beside a window
watching the wide white face of the moon
constant in her inconstancy

the soft darkness, the hard light
yielding, unyielding, yielding?

*

Don't pretend you can know me
she says
But we both know it is already too late

Metal / autumn

'[A] woman though born like a mouse may, it is feared, become a tiger.'

*

Smaller and therefore more humble, as the woman to the man, the younger to the older. And yet we crush the rock to extract the ounce of gold.

*

I want you to want. I want you to want other women to be like you. Do you want to save them? Or do you want to save them from being like you?

*

In 113 AD she accompanied her son, Cao Cheng, to his new post as a minor official in the east. Aged around fifty, she didn't know if she would ever see her home again. The poem she wrote, 'Travelling Eastwards', survives. In it she says (in translation, of course):

My heart hesitates as though it would fail me.
I pour out a cup of wine to relax my thoughts.
Suppressing my feelings, I sigh and blame myself:
I shall not need to dwell in nests, nor eat worms from dead trees.
Then how can I not encourage myself to press forward?
And further, am I different from other people?

*

I was going to write over your words.

I was going to write: 'Why does this feel like death to me? What's my problem? It's not as if I'm going to be homeless. What's my problem? Why do I always think I'm so special? Why can I not yield?'

*

We are always moving past ourselves
leaving our selves in their own shadows

*

Ban Zhao, Venerable Madame Cao, I struggled to find the right form for you, the right tone, the right box. Forgive me. I, like you, am an educated woman, though you are from a time when knowledge meant knowing things, not just knowing how to look them up.

Water / winter

 yin (jɪn) Also Yin, Yn. [Chinese *yīn* shade, feminine; the moon.]

 In Chinese philosophy, the feminine or negative principle

(characterized by dark, wetness, cold, passivity, disintegration, etc.) of the two opposing cosmic forces into which creative energy divides and whose fusion in physical matter brings the phenomenal world into being. Also attrib. or as adj., and transf. Cf. yang.

*

What women need to be philosophers
what women need
is education, so they know what people have said before them
and time to think, so they can build on it
or tear it down

*

'Yet only to teach men and not to teach women – is that not ignoring the essential relation between them? It is the rule to begin to teach children to read at the age of eight years, and by the age of fifteen they ought then to be ready for cultural training. Only why should it not be that girls' education as well as boys' be according to this principle?'

*

You already know that a drop of water, given time, can wash away stone
You already know that if you had patience like the water
all things would change in time
If you had the patience of the water
you would need the lifetime of water
You are sick of patience –
what is it but waiting and waiting
and being told you haven't yet waited long enough?

*

I am trying to read between your lines
Beneath the ink I hear your whispers and I think
you are saying: women are people too
I think
I am trying to forgive you for living in the past

Rocks

Envy might be green, but jealousy is red. A deep, furious red; a red you can lose your tongue in. There is a lot of pepper in jealousy. It burns in your throat, burns in your solar plexus and then burns right down in the pit of your stomach. A woman I knew, who had survived three husbands with barely a scratch, told me that feeling jealousy was a good thing because it showed you what you wanted. She also told me what someone had told her – someone who knew it by her own two feet: 'One step after another, out of the hard place.' I am not the kind of woman who wants to live a hard life.

Mr Andersen, you heartbreaker you

Oh Hans Christian Andersen, you tormentor
of children, creator of nightmares
The Little Mermaid always did me in
with her big love and her
enormous silence and giving up
her fishy tail for two legs
maybe to part them for
her sweet prince, but
relegated to the friend-zone
each shard of glass she stepped on
pricked a tiny hole into my
squishy little heart
And, really, if she'd just held on to her tongue
she could have sung him to her
reeled him in, drunk him down
One prince, on the rocks, coming up

*

And at the same time as the prince married the princess and the Little Mermaid turned into not even sea foam, but air, Andersen wrote to his friend Edvard Collin, who was also about to marry: 'I languish for you as for a pretty Calabrian wench . . . my sentiments for you are those of a woman.' Collin later wrote in his memoir, 'I found myself unable to respond to this love, and this caused the author much suffering.' Gosh, I can barely move for the shards of broken hearts beneath my feet.

I knew we were really supposed to take the audio guides
(at the Sisi Museum, Vienna)

but the resistance that stopped me
was the same resistance to being a tourist
that made me talk about 'the tourists' –
following the little flags held aloft by their guides
– like we were some other beings entirely

And so, rather than telling a story
the museum was a collection of objects
without explanation
Some the kinds of things you'd leave behind
in your old house when you moved
and didn't bother to sweep
as you left

There was a dental set, specially made
her hairbrush, a pair of gloves
that might once have encased her fingers
replicas of her hairstyles, jewellery
also replicas, reproductions of paintings
showing her wearing the jewellery and the dresses
which were also reproduced

While admiring the dresses, I got trapped
between the glass cases and the Spanish tour group
and the English one

Is this what it is like to visit a reliquary
to see little pieces of the saint, or the saint's

supposed possessions?
Holy, holy, and maybe healing
though I doubt you'd get much healing
from her: my teenage obsession

Painted on the walls were fragments of her poetry
which seem bad, though it's hard to tell in translation
It's all about her sorrow, sorrow
no hope for tomorrow and how she wants
to run, be free, but is caged
She did run though, and rode horses and travelled
in a railway carriage, of which this must be a replica
but without the audio guide I can't be sure

Even though I knew it was there
it wasn't picked out with a spotlight
and I'd walked right past the case when he said to me
'I don't know whether I should tell you this'
and when I turned around, there it was
behind me: a tiny thing, the file that killed her
punctured her heart, like Saint Teresa's arrows
but not really – there was no spiritual ecstasy
no floating up and into the clouds
just a real murder weapon and a small reproduction
of a newspaper report

How to die

From here there is nowhere else to go
only a question
of the journey, the route
and the hope of meandering
through a few more summers

We say we don't want suffering but often
given a chance, we will choose it
It all depends
on what the other choice is

Someone I trusted told me once that no one changes when they're dying
'You don't become what you're not'
And yet, we each have so many sides
how can *we* even say what is out of character?

My grandmother's cousin spent the day in town, walked home
up the hill, said to his wife, 'I feel a bit tired'
sat on his chair, took a nap
and never woke

My dad says he is not afraid
which has been a comfort, though it doesn't mean
he didn't fight, and he has won this round
I am not afraid because I refuse to even think of it

But the sky is so blue today
and the branches with their budding leaves
their shadows only adding to the light

In a poem of this title
you might justifiably have expected some advice
and it almost pains me to tell you
because I am full of wise advice at any hour of the day
that I must apologise

George Eliot: a life
A deconstructed biography

1. **The year of her birth, and the other**

1.1. Towards the end of 1819 – on the 22nd of November – Mary Anne Evans was born. 1819 is a very satisfying year, the most satisfying of the century; synonymous with orderly progress, like 1516, for example, or 2021. Others who were born in this illustrious year included art critic John Ruskin, composer Clara Schumann, poet Walt Whitman, novelist and sometime whaler Herman Melville; and, towering over them all, casting a shadow across the whole era with her name, was Princess Alexandrina: better known as Queen Victoria. Also in this year an English trading settlement was established in Singapore by Sir Stamford Raffles, who we now know of only thanks to his eponymous hotel. Spain ceded Florida to the United States, and Alabama became the twenty-second state. Fifteen people were killed and more than 600 injured in the Peterloo Massacre in Manchester, when cavalry charged at a crowd of more than 60,000 who had gathered to demand reform of parliamentary representation. The year is immortalised by Percy Bysshe Shelley in a political sonnet 'England in 1819' (unpublished until 1839, after his death), which paints a rather unflattering picture of the time: with a mad, dying, leech-like king, a corrupt army and Christless religion. John Keats gives up medicine for poetry, meets Fanny Brawne, the love of his life, and has his most poetically productive year. The Burlington Arcade, a shopping complex, opens in London (in which, in a tiny bookshop many years hence, our heroine will meet her match).

1.2. 1880 was a leap year. A general election is held in the United Kingdom; the Liberals beat the Conservatives and William Gladstone becomes prime minister for a second time. The Great Fog engulfs London for months. The University of London awards the first degrees to women in England. Gilbert and Sullivan's *The Pirates of Penzance* opens. The first electric streetlights are installed in Indiana. France annexes Tahiti. The First Boer War begins in Transvaal; the second Anglo–Afghan war rolls on. Cologne Cathedral is finally completed, 632 years after construction began. Greenwich Mean Time is adopted throughout Great Britain. Sixty-two coal miners die in a firedamp explosion in North Staffordshire, another 120 die in Monmouthshire, 164 in County Durham, 100 in Penygraig. Bushranger and folk hero Ned Kelly is hanged in Melbourne. In May, Marian Evans, writer, married John Cross, banker. On the 22nd of December George Eliot dies.

2.   On her names

2.1.   She started life as Mary Anne Evans, as christened by her father, one Robert Evans, land agent, and his wife, Christiana.

2.2.   At some point before 1837 she dropped an 'e' from her name, becoming instead Mary Ann Evans. It is possible the extra 'e' on Anne seemed to her an unnecessary flourish; she was, at that time, going through a particularly puritan phase. This version of her name first appears on the register for her sister's wedding, and so perhaps marks a new period of her life.

2.3.   In letters to certain friends she signed herself 'Polly', the name by which they knew her. Apparently Polly is a diminutive of Mary, which seems rather ridiculous until you learn it is by way of Molly. Her close friend Sara Hennell began calling her 'Pollian' – a play on Apollyon, the name of the monster in Revelations (in Greek anyway – in Hebrew it's Abaddon), who also appears in *The Pilgrim's Progress*. Why a friend would want to compare her to a 'foul fiend' I am not quite sure, and whether in jest or cruelty; but, by all reports, she *was* very badly dressed for most of her life, especially during her puritan years.

2.4.   She was known to call herself 'Medusa'. I guess that's OK, in the way it's OK for you to insult your own home town, but are upset when anyone else does.

2.5. Another name she used for letter-writing purposes – in those days between school and marriage, when letters are the lifeline of a young woman smothered by the duties of home and family – was 'Clematis', which, in the language of flowers, means mental beauty. Her former teacher, Miss Lewis, was dubbed 'Veronica', for fidelity in friendship; while another friend, Martha, got to be 'Ivy', for constancy. I may be wrong in assuming that it was Mary Ann who got to assign the flower names, but it has her fingerprints all over it.

2.6. After her father died, Mary Ann lived for a time in Geneva with the D'Albert Durade family. She came to address Mme D'Albert Durade as 'Maman', Mamma, and became like one of the family: 'and I am baby enough to find that a great addition to my happiness'. The D'Albert Durades called her 'Minie'.

2.7. In 1851, when she left provincial Warwickshire for London, she marked the transition by again altering her name – this time to Marian, which seems to me a bit sterner than Mary Ann, and perhaps sterner stuff is what she needed for this new city.

2.8. In the unlikely – OK, impossible – event that we should ever meet, not only would I be flummoxed about what name to use to address her, I am not at all sure we would get along. (I fear she would think me too frivolous, and I might find her a condescending know-it-all.) I have long suspected that might be the case with all my literary heroes: Sylvia Plath, Katherine Mansfield, Anne Sexton, Virginia Woolf, to name just a few. Perhaps this is why, when I had an opportunity to meet, and have my books signed by, Margaret Atwood, to whom I devoted several years of my life and a master's thesis, I decided to not join the queue.

2.9. When she started living with George Lewes, despite the fact that they did not and could not marry, not in a legal sense anyway, Marian began signing herself as 'Marian Evans Lewes'. As far as she was concerned, they were married in the ways that mattered, and, besides, it helped enormously with landladies.

2.10. Marian isn't just a more plain spelling of Mary Ann (and Mary Anne), it also denotes being of or related to the Blessed Virgin Mary, the Queen of Heaven, the mother of Christ, the Madonna (as opposed to the other). Marian, surrounded by (almost always only male) admirers at the Sunday afternoon salons she and Lewes held in their home, did apparently rather resemble the Queen of Heaven; and perhaps that is why Lewes took to sometimes calling her 'Madonna'. (We can safely assume that it had nothing to do with the never-aging pop star of our own time.)

2.11. But mainly he seems to have called her 'Polly' (refer 2.3. above).

2.12. We know her by the name we know her because we really only know her because of her words. But she didn't take it up immediately. Her first published fiction, 'The Sad Fortunes of the Reverend Amos Barton', was published anonymously, and her publisher John Blackwood, who did not yet know the author's identity, resorted to calling her 'the Author of Amos Barton'.

2.13. She knew, given her circumstances – a woman living with a man who was not her husband (and in fact was, legally at any rate, someone else's) – she must not write as herself, or at least not under her own name. We also shouldn't underestimate the advantage one can gain when wearing not only a mask, but a male mask. She told John Cross she chose it because 'George was Mr Lewes's Christian name, and Eliot was a good, mouth-filling, easily pronounced word.' It has been suggested that the surname, as well as the first, honours her beloved partner: 'To L---- I owe it.'

2.14. Despite 'Marian', despite 'George', she still had some need for Mary Ann, because in his will George Lewes left everything (except the copyright of his works, which he left to his surviving son) to 'Mary Ann Evans, spinster'.

2.15. Following Lewes's death she was finally able to, or rather had to, take his name – changing it by deed poll to Mary Ann Evans Lewes to be able to access a bank account in Lewes's name, which she had inherited. Her reasons were not self-interested – the money was for a new scholarship for a student of physiology, open to both men and women.

2.16. At Highgate Cemetery is the grave of a woman we have not yet met: Mary Ann Cross, wife of banker John Cross. They had wed eighteen months after the death of George Lewes, and were married for only seven months before Mary Ann died of kidney failure. John Cross, who Marian and George Lewes had fondly called 'nephew', was forty when they married; Mary Ann was sixty. They fell in love while reading *The Divine Comedy* together as a distraction from their griefs: her partner, his mother. It is this wife's name on the gravestone, because it is Mary Ann's body that lies there. 'George Eliot' is included in quote marks; however, the body of George Eliot, surely, is not there, because it was made not of flesh and blood, but of paper and words.

3. **On her head**
3.1. A leading phrenologist of the day, George Combe of Edinburgh, on seeing a cast of Mary Ann Evans's head, thought it was of a man's – presumably it was rather large.

3.2. Later, Combe had the pleasure of examining Mary Ann's head in the flesh, and in the bone, and declared it: 'extraordinary'. He admired her 'very large brain, the anterior lobe is remarkable for length, breadth, and height, the coronal region is large, the front rather predominating'.

3.2.1. I think this may have been a polite, phrenological, way of saying that she was the smartest guy in the room.

3.3. When Marian shacked up with Lewes, Combe was 'mortified and distressed' that his admirable subject, with so fine a head, could be capable of such immorality. He asked a mutual friend if there was insanity in her family – surely the only logical explanation.

4. On her appearance

4.1. People go on and on about how 'plain' – by which they mean ugly – George Eliot was, including Mary Ann Evans herself, and every biographer since. But really, even though the remaining portraits might be flattering, they suggest that she was basically a fairly ordinary-looking woman with a slightly larger than average nose. I mean, her face might not have been fashionable at the time, but if she was walking past you down Lambton Quay, say, or Queen Street, you'd walk right past her without even a thought.

4.2. She had abundant brown hair, which, when she was younger, may have been blonde. Her eyes were grey-blue and heavily lidded. Her face was said to be long and equine.

4.3. My friend A, who, in the past and perhaps on bad days, thought (quite incorrectly) that she was not beautiful, tells me about how, when first coming across George Eliot as a precocious pre-teen, she got angry for underappreciated women everywhere, because of everyone going on about her appearance rather than her achievements. 'I mean, they don't do that to male writers, do they? *Do they?*'

4.4. It would appear that I am *also* going on about her appearance.

4.5. I would like to think that we are past this, but just the other week Colleen McCullough died, and (though I haven't actually read any of her books) I was appalled that the first paragraph in an obituary in a major Australian newspaper didn't comment on the fact that she was a neuroscientist as well as a wildly successful author, but rather said, basically, that she was fat and ugly, but by some miracle she still managed to get laid.

4.5.1. I think that a discussion of, or rather a collective rant about, 4.5. above was what sparked the conversation, or perhaps confession, at 4.3. above.

4.6. Immediately after 4.3. I told A what I am about to tell you – not to diminish the seriousness of 4.3. and 4.5., etc., but perhaps in an attempt at equal-opportunity judgementalism – that the looks of George Lewes were also frequently remarked upon.

4.6.1. George Lewes was, in his time, famously ugly. He was known as 'the ape' and 'hairy Lewes' by the Carlyles (Thomas and Jane – see 8.6.), and Edmund Gosse described him as 'hirsute, rugged, satyr-like', which I guess isn't necessarily all bad.

4.6.2. Marian herself, the love of his life, described George Lewes after their first meeting in a tiny bookshop run by William Jeffs in Burlington Arcade in 1851 (as alluded to in 1.1.), as 'a sort of miniature Mirabeau in appearance'. Mirabeau is an art deco apartment building on a street where my husband once lived when he was just my boyfriend, but apparently Mirabeau was also a French politician during the revolution who was known for his pockmarked face, and presumably it was this Mirabeau to whom Marian was referring. But it also means in French, 'beautiful sight', and who are we to say . . .

4.7. Despite their looks, both Marian Evans and George Lewes – and Honoré Gabriel Riqueti, Comte de Mirabeau for that matter, and many plain people all through time, all over the world – managed to get laid, and be loved, even adored.

4.8. But, back to George Eliot: Henry James wrote of her after their first meeting in a letter to his father: 'She is magnificently ugly – deliciously hideous.' He continued, 'She has a low forehead, a dull grey eye, a vast pendulous nose, a huge mouth, full of uneven teeth and a chin and jaw-bone qui n'en finissent pas.' (You might understand French, but for those of us who don't, Google Translate says that means 'that never end'.) James, who at that stage was a young and handsome twenty-six-year-old, then went on to say, 'Now in this vast ugliness resides a most powerful beauty which, in a very few minutes steals forth and charms the mind, so that you end as I ended, in falling in love with her.'

5. **On art**
5.1. Before she began writing her own fiction, though not long before, she wrote, 'The greatest benefit we owe to the artist, whether painter, poet, or novelist, is the extension of our sympathies ... Art is the nearest thing to life; it is the mode of amplifying experience and extending our contact with our fellow-men beyond the bounds of our personal lot.'

6. **A chronological list and brief outlines of her novels**
6.1. *Adam Bede*, 1859. Nice girls get the guy, bad girls get transported – if they're lucky.

6.2. *The Mill on the Floss*, 1860. Girl is smarter than her brother and it all ends in tears.

6.3. *Silas Marner: The Weaver of Raveloe*, 1861. Hermity weaver gets gold, loses gold, gets golden-haired girl-child instead, thus losing hermityness, but then gets gold back again.

6.4. *Romola*, 1863. Scholarly Florentine woman makes a bad marriage, but at least she doesn't get burned at the stake like Savonarola.

6.5. *Felix Holt, the Radical*, 1866. There's some reforming goin' on in provincial England.

6.6. *Middlemarch*, 1871–1872. Idealistic young wealthy woman and idealistic young impecunious doctor get married, but not to each other.

6.7. *Daniel Deronda*, 1876. Two novels that have yet to be properly introduced to each other. Cynical young woman tries to get the attention of rich neighbour

– so far so second-rate-Jane-Austen, but no, now it's more like what might happen after the Jane Austen novel ends, and now there's an unexpected twist of Jewish mysticism, all hinging on an arrogant and manipulative man – and he's the nice one. Fascinating but flawed, which is probably true of all George Eliot novels, with the exception of 6.6., which, in my recollection at least, is basically perfect.

7.   Some of the places in which she lived

7.1.   South Farm, Arbury Estate, near Nuneaton, Warwickshire, 1819–1820. A smallish stone farmhouse where Mary Anne Evans was born.

7.2.   Griff House, near Nuneaton, 1820–1841. A large Georgian brick house to which Mary Anne moved with her family when she was a few months old. There were four acres of gardens, fruit trees, stables, four living rooms, eight bedrooms and three attics. One of these attics was her refuge, to which she would escape to dream, or think, or stare out the window. You can visit it if you want to – not because it's become one of those National Trust writer shrines, but because it's now a pub. The pokies perch on the flagstones of the entrance hall, pool tables are in the dining room and the parlour has become a sports bar.

7.3.   Mrs Wallington's School, Nuneaton, 1828–1832. Unlike Virginia Woolf, whose father did not believe that girls should be educated outside the home, Mary Anne was of a class both high enough and low enough to be sent to school to get a halfway decent education.

7.4.   The Miss Franklin's School for Girls, Coventry, 1832–1835. A schoolmate remembered her as a clever but shy girl, who regularly rushed out of the room in tears (compare with 12.1. below).

7.5.   Bird Grove, Foleshill, Coventry, 1841–1849. Mary Ann lived here with her widowed, retired father, after her brother Isaac had taken over their father's position as agent for Sir Francis Newdigate and had married, giving Griff

House a new mistress. Mary Ann, who had, since the death of her mother when she was aged sixteen, been the housekeeper and mistress of the house, was toppled from her pedestal and 'severed from all the ties that have hither to given my existence the semblance of a usefulness beyond that of making up the requisite quantum of animal matter in the universe', i.e. she was a bit miffed. As well as getting them out of the house, another reason for Mary Ann and her father's move to this fashionable edge of Coventry was to display her to potential husbands. Robert Evans very nearly gave up the house during 'The Holy War', when Mary Ann confessed that she had lost her faith and refused to go to church. They reached a compromise (she would accompany him to church, and her private beliefs were her own problem) and this impasse survived until his death.

7.6.   The home of Monsieur and Madame D'Albert Durade, Geneva, 1849–1850. After her father's death, Mary Ann accompanied her friends Charles and Cara Bray on a trip to the Continent – as Europe is often called by the British, from their small island at the edge. She – bravely? desperately? – stayed on in Geneva afterwards, at first in a pension, but later in the home of the D'Albert Durades, a middle-aged couple (see also 2.6.).

7.7.   142 The Strand, London, 1851–1853. 'My return to England is anything but joyous to me', Mary Ann wrote, and her family didn't seem that delighted about it either. So, without a place to be, or a role to play, she decided to move to London and try her hand at journalism. Marian boarded at the large home of John Chapman, publisher; Susanna, his wife; their children; Elisabeth Tilley, the children's governess, who was also Chapman's mistress; and assorted other lodgers. There was a gap in her residence at 142 when wife and mistress banded together to evict Marian, who had also likely been seduced by the amorous Chapman. She was allowed to return some months later – because Chapman needed her talents for his newly acquired *Westminster Review*, of which she became the anonymous editor – on condition that Chapman did not return to her bed.

7.8. 21 Cambridge Street, London, 1853–1854. Marian moved to a lodging on her own, presumably so she could have more privacy with her most frequent gentleman caller: one George Lewes.

7.9. 62A Kaufgasse, Weimar, Germany, 1854–1855. The house of Frau Münderloh. The apartment had three rooms: Marian's bedroom, George Lewes's bedroom and a sitting room, which could only be reached through Lewes's bedroom. An English visitor, one Mr Tait, in a letter (to our phrenologist friend, George Combe, who you might remember from 3.) draws no definite conclusion from this, but notes, 'The circumstances certainly are suspicious.'

7.10. 8 Park Shot, Richmond, 1855–1859. After their return from many months in Germany, and a couple of months in other locations, Marian and George settled into lodgings on the second floor of Miss Croft's quiet and secluded ivy-covered Georgian house, which was handy to the railway station. It is now, apparently, the site of the magistrates' court.

7.11. Holly Lodge, Wimbledon Park Road, Wandsworth, 1859–1860. Having made a bit of money from their various works of literature (*Sea-side Studies* for George L and *Adam Bede* for George E) they set up house in this semi-detached. Marian found the house oppressive and did not enjoy housekeeping, or in fact Wandsworth, writing to a friend who lived nearby, 'I dislike Wandsworth and should think with unmitigated regret of our coming here if it were not for you.'

7.12. 16 Blandford Square, Marylebone, London, 1860–1863. When Lewes's oldest son, Charles, finished school, on the advice of Anthony Trollope – writer and famous employee of the Post Office – he took the civil service exam and also became an employee of the Post Office. The move back to London was mainly so it was easier for Charles, who was now living with them, to get to work on time.

7.13. The Priory, 21 North Bank, Regent's Park, London, 1863–1880. Marian and George purchased this large standalone house for £2000, and then spared no expense in having it redecorated and modernised by designer Owen Jones. Here, they began their Sunday afternoon salons, which many notable persons attended, such as Robert Browning, Charles Dickens, Ivan Turgenev, Charles Darwin, Henry James and Alfred Tennyson. A few progressive women braved the visit, but most of the gentlemen did not bring their wives.

7.14. Cottage, Redhill, Surrey, 1872. Work on *Middlemarch* was taking its toll on George Eliot, and so, as they often did, she and Lewes rented a cottage in the country, where they could be, as he said in a letter to Charles, 'shut out from the world amid fields'.

7.15. The Heights, Whiteley, Surrey, 1877–1880. After many years of looking for a country place, John Cross found them this substantial red-brick house with land and views, which was not too far from where Cross lived with his mother. They paid just under £5000 and set about improving and redecorating it. They had intended to sell The Priory and settle in the country permanently, but, after finding it a little cold, they used it only as a summer residence. The house was built in Arts and Crafts style, and set in tiles on the north and east walls is a quote from *King Lear*: 'Have more than thou shewest. Speak less than thou knowest.'

7.16. 4 Cheyne Walk, Chelsea, London, 1880. In April, as soon as Marian agreed to marry him, Cross took a lease on this Georgian terrace house on the Embankment (which was purchased in 2015 for £17 million by billionaire and former mayor of New York Michael Bloomberg, who denied rumours that it would become a base for him to campaign for the mayoralty of London). However, Marian and John did not move in until the 3rd of December, after their honeymoon and time for the new house to be made ready. They lived there together for just three weeks before Marian died, leaving Johnny 'alone in this new House we meant to be so happy in'.

8. **A small selection of her most interesting friends and acquaintances**

8.1. Elizabeth Evans née Tomlinson was full of love for mankind, which grated on the puritan sensibilities of her young niece Mary Anne. Elizabeth was a Methodist lay preacher, called to spread the good news. When the church hierarchy decided women should not preach, she and her husband, Mary Anne's father's brother, joined a breakaway group with fewer restrictions. Readers of George Eliot's first novel, *Adam Bede*, might recall an incident where Dinah, a lay preacher, ministers to young Hetty Sorrel, who then confesses to killing her illegitimate child. This was based on the experiences of Elizabeth, who then, however, accompanied the young woman to her execution the next morning, while Hetty gets away with transportation to Australia.

8.2. Pivotal to Mary Ann's life was Charles Bray – ribbon manufacturer, amateur phrenologist, social reformer, freethinker – and his wife Cara. Charles was a leonine man with a thick mane of hair that looks in photographs like it is being blown back by a medium-sized wind machine. He and Cara lived at Rosehill, their house in Coventry, where everyone who was 'a little cracked' was said to visit – and where they would likely have met the Brays' good friend: Miss Mary Ann Evans. He, in fine tradition, kept a mistress, and for a time he and Cara, who had no children, cared for one of the six children he had fathered elsewhere. He owned the *Coventry Herald*, and authored several books, including *The Education of the Body: An Address to the Working Classes*; *Psychological and Ethical Definitions on a Physiological Basis*; and *The Industrial Employment of Women: Being a Comparison Between the Condition of the People in the Watch Trade in Coventry, in Which Women are Not Employed, and the People in the Ribbon Trade*.

8.3. In the 1850s John Chapman (who you may recall from 7.7. above) was the go-to publisher of most freethinking authors, from dissenters to atheists, reformers and feminists to transcendentalists and psychologists, many of whom met each other through him and his soirées. He was the editor of the

Westminster Review for decades, long after Marian bailed on him, keeping it going with his own gristle and other people's money. Despite these achievements, he is generally thought of as a terrible businessman, a mediocre writer and a bit of a fool. He went on to become a medical doctor specialising in women's gynaecological health and the inventor of Dr Chapman's patented 'Spine-bags', to heat or ice the spine. A cad, possibly; a ladies' man, probably; a charmer, certainly. Even in old age, he was said to be beautiful.

8.4. If it wasn't for Freud, Herbert Spencer, psychologist, philosopher, sociologist and train engineer, would probably be known for much more than being the guy who rejected George Eliot. Like many Victorian thinkers, of which he was one of the most important, he's been swept away in a wave of unpopularity. He wrote many books about many things, though no one reads them now. Inventor of the phrase 'survival of the fittest' (though Darwin usually gets the credit). He believed in the equality of the sexes, and so presumably required beauty in men as much as he did in women (hence the rejection of Marian). In his old age, when he had become more conservative, he shared a house with two sisters, and refused to dine with them when their plain friend came to visit. They recalled him as an irascible man who liked to wear a knitted garment of his own design, nicknamed the 'woolly bear', that incorporated boots, trousers and coat – so possibly we should be celebrating him as the inventor of the onesie.

8.5. Harriet Martineau was one of the many women writers of the age who were perfectly happy to publish under their own names. Celebrated novelist, sociologist, political economist, feminist, translator, and apologist for mesmerism and 'philosophical atheism' – the latter beginning a feud with her favourite brother, Unitarian minister James Martineau, because her freethinking was even more extreme than his. She broke off contact with Marian when the latter snuck off to Weimar with Lewes, which was hardly surprising as she did the same to Elizabeth Barrett when she eloped with Browning. Harriet wrote her autobiography in 1855, when she thought she was about to die, to be published posthumously; but in fact she lived until 1876, which saved a lot of people a lot of heartache, because they were no longer alive to read the mean things she'd said about them.

8.6. Thomas Carlyle should not really be in this section, as he was neither a friend nor acquaintance of Marian's, though he was friendly with Lewes. After the Weimar incident, when other people were jettisoning Marian from their Christmas card lists, Carlyle and his wife Jane chose to simply not become acquainted with this 'strong-minded woman'. Nevertheless, Carlyle is peppered through biographies of Eliot, and perhaps of all Victorians, because he was ubiquitous. Everywhere you turn in Victorian England (and Victorian Scotland for that matter, as he was in fact Scottish), there he is! It is perhaps a little hard to tell why now – unlike other, lesser, Victorians, his fame has not carried across into our time, but he was *the* preeminent thinker – mathematician, philosopher, novelist, historian and social critic. The Simon Schama of Victorian Britain, if you will, but more so.

8.6.1. I confess to a particular reason for including Carlyle, despite his lack of friendship with Eliot, because when I started saying, around age eight, that I was going to be a writer, my mother said, 'Like Thomas Carlyle', who, I was given to understand, was an illustrious ancestor of ours. I soon found out that was not strictly true, as he was actually her great great great uncle, so there was no direct line (and he did not in fact have a direct line of his own – due, at least in part, to his alleged impotence), but surely we must share some genetic material? I'm sure it is my granny's nose I see in a silhouette of Carlyle's mother, my granny who always carried peppermints to relieve the dyspepsia from which she, like Carlyle, suffered.

8.7. Painter Barbara Leigh Smith Bodichon strides out of the pages of other people's biographies in her sturdy boots and the skirt she has shortened by four inches to make walking across country easier. She shines. People fell in love with her, I fell in love with her; she is the kind of woman who sends you to abebooks.com to order out-of-print biographies and wonder at how someone so marvellous has been forgotten. She grew up in the 'tabooed family' – her wealthy Unitarian father, Benjamin Smith, had not married her mother, a milliner, for reasons uncertain (the scandal of the class difference would have been small compared to the scandal of the unmarriage), and he brought up his brood of children when she died. He had them all educated, both boys and girls, and gave them an equal fortune when they turned twenty-one. Her friend, Pre-Raphaelite painter Dante Gabriel Rossetti, described Barbara as 'blessed with large rations of tin, fat, enthusiasm, and golden hair.' She made good use of her 'tin' (and her enthusiasm, charm and intelligence) in her various campaigns – educational, political, feminist. A staunch advocate of sisterhood, she ran schools, founded and funded the *English Women's Journal*, started petitions, wrote pamphlets about the rights of women under the law and founded Girton, a women's college, which eventually became part of Cambridge. Basically, she founded the organised women's movement in England. She decided against a sexual relationship with John Chapman (8.3. above), despite his insistence that it would be good for her health, and then shocked even her liberal family by marrying Eugène Bodichon, an eccentric French doctor living in Algiers. Possibly her first love was painting landscapes, for which she was much-admired by her contemporaries. Now, *she* is someone I would like to have met (compare and contrast with 2.8.).

8.8. George Lewes's father was a mediocre poet who had a wife and children, began a second family with George's mum, and then left the lot of them for Bermuda. An unconventional beginning for a man who didn't care much for convention, and was more interested in truth, beauty, and a bit of fun. Lewes junior considered medicine, tried acting, then settled on writing for his living. With his best friend Thornton Hunt he founded a newspaper, *The Leader*. He wrote articles and books on subjects ranging from philosophy to biology, literature to psychology – like many of his age, his interests were broad, though some thought him shallow and fickle. His final work, *Problems of Life and Mind*, which he jokingly called 'the key to all psychologies' in reference to

Casaubon's doomed key to all mythologies in *Middlemarch*, was unfinished when he died in 1878. However, unlike Dorothea, Marian Evans spent the first months after her beloved's death ordering and completing the manuscript, which was published in four volumes.

8.9. We don't know much about Agnes Lewes née Jarvis, except that she seemed to be a genial person, and never caused trouble for her estranged husband George Lewes or his new partner Marian Evans, except in the financial support they continued to send her for their whole lives. We know that she was only eighteen when she married George, and that their marriage was open and unconventional, in a Shelleyan free-love kind of way. We suspect that was probably George's idea. We know their friends thought they were very happy together. We know she had at least four children with George's best friend (Thornton Hunt) after the three (surviving) with George. And we know George let them all have his last name, so they would not be illegitimate, which meant that in the eyes of the law he had 'condoned', and so everyone feels sorry for him because he couldn't divorce the adulteress. I can't help but feel that the rules have changed mid-game. We know she lived around the corner from George and Marian in Kensington. We know she lived until 1902, outlasting them all. We don't know how she felt about any of this.

9. **On why I am writing this**

9.1. When I began, before momentum took over, I frequently asked this of myself: why am I writing about George Eliot? Why am I writing about a woman who lived more than 100 years ago in a country on the other side of the world where a few of my ancestors are from, and which I'm not sure I even like very much – I mean the country, but perhaps also the person (see also 2.8.). Especially as the reason I didn't like England very much was because when I got to London and saw all those places that had been the living contents of my head – that I'd read about my whole life, where all these writers and painters, who seemed more familiar to me than my own grandparents, had lived – and found that they were really real, I also realised that I meant nothing to them. I had no claim on this place, this land, this culture that had colonised my mind with its stories.

9.2. I suppose, having asked myself that question, I should make some attempt to answer it.

9.3. Or should I? I was once told that the difference between art and design is that design solves problems, while art asks questions. This asks some questions, and I doubt this will solve anyone's problems, so perhaps this is art? But maybe that is a false dichotomy. Maybe design *can* ask questions. Maybe art *can* solve problems. Or at least make tentative suggestions?

9.3.1. The woman who told me that (9.3. above) was an artist who was always told her art was 'too designy', and who had previously been a designer who'd been told her designs were 'too arty'. Like many people, she had entered art school wanting to become a painter and left as a conceptual video artist. I saw one of her exhibitions and remember only a woman, in slow motion on a mechanical bull, who seemed to float as if the air was water. But that has nothing to do with the topic at hand.

9.4. In any case, I don't yet know the answer to 9., but I think it might have something to do with Dorothea.

9.4.1. Is Dorothea, the heroine of George Eliot's greatest novel, *Middlemarch*, an idealised version of Marian Evans? Like Marian, she's intelligent and (arguably) moral. Unlike George Eliot, she is beautiful and wealthy and many men want to marry her.

9.4.2. Is Marian Evans the idealised version of Dorothea? Dorothea longs for a marriage of minds, but finds only disappointment. Dorothea longs to do something, but manages only to be a 'foundress of nothing' and someone's good wife. An anticlimax, resting in an unvisited (albeit fictional) tomb.

Meanwhile, Marian, as we are discovering, strode out into the world. Made a name. Lived a life.

9.4.3. But I digress! And anyway, probably this would be better placed with 10.7. below – feel free to cut and paste.

9.5. Surely you have, by now, forgotten the question, and so I feel at liberty to remark that *Middlemarch*, with a wide cast of characters in a provincial English town, offers us a range of ways to live, and philosophies to live by. But I am not sure I am convinced by any of them.

9.6. People are endlessly fascinating. Especially the fascinating ones.

10. On the 'Woman Question'

10.1. What even *was* the question? What are women? What should women be? Are women equal to men? *How* to make women equal to men? How to stop women complaining about their lack of equality with men? All of the above?

10.2. You could perhaps divide exceptional women – the women who, despite the obstacles of lack of education, opportunity and respect, manage to rise in their field – into two types: the ones who want to take other women with them, and the ones who don't.

10.2.1. You could say the same about exceptional men.

10.2.2. Referring back to 10.2., which was George Eliot?

10.3. Because of her disrespectability (i.e. living in sin), much of Marian's social life was reduced to men, and only the odd adventurous woman. Did she mind this? Probably not (refer to the end of 11.6.). Writer Eliza Lynn Linton said of her, with a tablespoonful of spite, 'She was always the goddess on her pedestal' (refer also 2.10.).

10.4. Marian refused to sign Barbara Bodichon's 1867 petition for women to gain the vote. When asked by Clementia Taylor to help with the suffrage campaign, she replied that while she did want to see women educated equally with men, she did not agree that much would be achieved from 'a particular measure'. She thought the enfranchisement of women would be 'an extremely doubtful good'.

10.4.1. I am reminded here of another exceptional and scandalous woman, another writer, another George: George Sand, who, when nominated (without her consent) to stand for the French National Assembly, refused, firmly disassociated herself with the women pushing for change and said, 'I don't see why, as things presently stand, women should be in such a rush to participate directly in political life.'

10.5. About two weeks before she began writing her own fiction, Marian published (anonymously) a rather unsisterly attack on female fiction writers: 'Silly Novels by Lady Novelists'. She categorises the various sub-species of silly novels written by women and uses generous quotations to illustrate their ridiculousness. She does admit that some of her favourite novelists are women, such as Currer Bell (Charlotte Brontë), but leaves the impression that only exceptional women are worthwhile. After that, it is hardly surprising that she felt the pressure of being constantly judged and constantly wanting.

10.6. George Eliot was so good at creating a male persona that a man, Joseph Liggins of Nuneaton, convinced many that *he* was the author of her novels. However, Charles Dickens suspected from the first that the author was a woman, or, if not, he said, 'I believe no man ever before had the art of making himself, mentally, so like a woman, since the world began.'

10.7. Sometimes my friend A talks about a 'writer's crack', much like a builder's crack – 'Excuse me, your id is showing' – meaning they've revealed more about themselves than they probably realised, and it's a little bit awkward for everyone concerned. In reading George Eliot's novels, it is hard to not notice the blonde women who are pretty but rather insipid, and range from stupid to merely average intelligence. But worse are the dark-haired, brown-complexioned women, who are underestimated but brilliant and passionate, and generally beautiful. One of these, Maggie, the heroine of *The Mill on the Floss* – the character seen by many as the most autobiographical of Eliot's creations – starts out as an ugly duckling, but grows into a beauty, steals the affections of a man from her blonde cousin (though can't go through with it because of her good nature) and makes up with her estranged brother whom she adored (refer 11.3. below). So obvious is the wish fulfilment that I would have shuffled in embarrassment and coughed quietly if I hadn't been crying so hard.

10.7.1. But the fact is, and I don't want to give you spoilers, that for such an extraordinary woman she sure did create some disappointing female characters. Even the heroines don't strike out – they give up, they stop, they enclose themselves in family, they stand behind, they cease, they die. They found nothing.

10.7.2. Did she think that she was too exceptional to be used as a model for her characters? Did she think that while *she* was good enough to be involved in intellectual life, and *she* could probably even be trusted to vote, the same could not be said for her inferior sisters?

10.8. In a letter to her friend, Jane Senior, she said, 'There is no subject on which I am more inclined to hold my peace and learn, than on the "Woman Question".'

11. On love

11.1. Everyone goes on about the incompatibility of Dorothea and Casaubon, but when I first read the start of *Middlemarch* (second year English lit, which is also why I only read the first part – it was the last book of the course and I could either finish reading it, or study for my exams; I made my choice – same deal for *War and Peace*) I could see why Dorothea was attracted to Casaubon. I myself felt a little attracted to Casaubon, because surely it's the mind and not the skin that matters. We're always being told that. A year or so later when I watched the TV miniseries (Rufus Sewell et al.), having still not returned to the book, I was bewildered at how badly Dorothea and Casaubon's marriage goes. I felt betrayed, but also foolish to have thought it could ever have been otherwise. When I *did* read *Middlemarch* – all the way through this time – after a decade or so of my own marriage (to say it has been a 'happy marriage' sounds so generic, so clichéd, so cutesy pie, and whether the marriage has made us happy, or whether we have made the marriage happy (perhaps a bit of both?) – but being with him is one of the things in my life that makes me the happiest), I felt I understood better what went wrong for Dorothea and Casaubon, who both start out with such optimism and lofty intentions; and it seemed less incompatibility and more lack – of understanding, of communication, of kindness, of a willingness to reach out to each other at the same time. One is always reaching, the other always shrinking back.

11.2. I don't think of myself as a romantic. I think you can, for example, live a very good life as a single person, and being alone is better than being in a bad relationship – and here I am feeling the need to justify (and perhaps overstate?) my lack of romanticism, or rather balance out what I am about to say, because I find this a bit awkward: but I feel that love has made me. I expect you can't tell, because you are reading this in an instant, but it took me a long time to write that sentence. I got distracted. I procrastinated. I stared at the walls for a while, as if I can't bear to look it in the face. But what am I doing in here anyway? I'm just the biographer.

11.2.1. But George Eliot was made by love too. Marian basked in it. She blossomed. This was the woman who once wrote to Herbert Spencer (8.4.) – a close friend who, not feeling that way inclined, had warned her not to fall in love with him (whether that advice was belated, or whether it in fact precipitated Marian's ardour I am not sure). Marian responded: 'I felt disappointed rather than "hurt" that you should not have sufficiently divined my character to perceive how remote it is from my habitual state of mind to imagine that anyone is falling in love with me.' But, not long after, someone did.

11.3. Marian, who had been no one's special person for thirty-five years, flourished under the sun that was George Lewes's love. She glowed. Even though it meant a scandal. Even though it meant no respectable woman could visit her. Even though it meant her brother forbade the rest of her family from contacting her, and she never saw him again. I wouldn't say she didn't care, but she didn't care enough. Not enough to stop.

11.4. In her journal, on New Year's Eve 1857, after three and a half years with Lewes, Marian wrote: 'my happiness has deepened too: the blessedness of a perfect love and union grows daily . . . Few women, I fear have had such reason as I have to think the long sad years of youth were worth living for the sake of middle age.' And, even further into her middle age, on New Year's Eve 1870, she wrote, 'In my private lot I am unspeakably happy, loving and beloved.'

11.5. I am trying to think of some other examples of happy relationships. Queen Victoria and Prince Albert? Though, of course, he died, and she was miserable and everyone had to wear black. Virginia Woolf and Leonard were pretty happy – but again, until her death. Marie and Pierre Curie? Actually, all I know about them is that they did experiments together, and died, one after the other, from radiation poisoning from those experiments. If divorce doesn't get you, death will. Loss: the inevitable price of love.

11.5.1. I couldn't think of many more (happy relationships that is), and it may be my meagre knowledge, but I think that's because happy relationships don't tend to make good stories – or what we are told are good stories: with dramatic conflict, passion, striking out for freedom and so forth. But drama can always be found, and there are other ways to develop.

11.5.2. Marian *did* develop. When she met Lewes she was already a well-regarded journalist and editor of the *Westminster Review* – though her writing was published anonymously, everyone knew it was her. Everyone who mattered, anyway. But it was Lewes who encouraged her to write fiction. He encouraged her in a way that wouldn't put too much pressure on her, set her expectations low enough that she could write at all, and then praised her enough that she would keep on. He told her she was a genius. He censored her mail so she would never see a bad review. I can't say I approve of censoring people's mail, unless they ask for it, which perhaps she had. And it is also possible he just encouraged her to write fiction because they needed some more cash – he did have a wife and children to support after all – but without George Lewes we might not have George Eliot, and without George Eliot…

11.6. Of course Lewes wasn't the only person who loved Marian Evans. Or Mary Ann. Or even George. Among Eliot's several ardent admirers was Edith Simcox, a much younger woman who met Marian in her later years. Edith was a writer, feminist and trade unionist who ran a shirt-making factory. Her admiration went beyond friendship, through the sexual and right into the religious: 'Day by day let me begin and end by looking to Her for guidance and rebuke.' When Edith got too amorous, Marian let her know that she didn't feel 'that way' about women, and that: 'the friendship and intimacy of men was more to her'.

11.7. John Cross loved her, and she loved him. I know there are rumours about his intentions in marrying her, and mean things have been said about why he might have jumped out the window of their hotel room into Venice's Grand Canal on their honeymoon (he said the bad drains, extreme heat and exhaustion from sightseeing made him thoroughly ill – and surely any mismatch of sexual expectations would have been uncovered earlier in the honeymoon). But he was Dante, she his Beatrice.

11.7.1. Marian had been very secretive about her impending marriage to Cross, probably wisely as it bamboozled many, and was, for some, more scandalous than her relationship with a married man. She had written letters of explanation to a selection of close friends, which they were to receive after she'd left on her honeymoon. Barbara Bodichon (8.7.) might have expected to receive one (and would have if it had not been left unposted in a drawer, where it was discovered several months later); nevertheless, she did not take offence and, after learning of the nuptials from the newspaper, sent her congratulations:

> My dear I hope and think you will be happy.
>
> Tell Johnny Cross I should have done exactly what he has done if you would have let me and I had been a man.
>
> You see I know all love is so different that I do not see it unnatural to love in new ways – not to be unfaithful to any memory.
>
> If I knew Mr Lewes he would be glad as I am that you have a new friend.

12. On screaming

12.1. In March 1840, during her puritan phase, Mary Ann went to a party given by an old family friend. Presumably disapproving of all the dancing, laughing, flirting and general fun-having of the other guests, or perhaps attracted by them, she first retreated to the edges and complained of a headache; but then she started screaming hysterically. One biographer suggests it was because of an internal war between piousness and music, which was making her want to get outside of herself and dance. But perhaps she just didn't like loud music and crowds.

12.2. Another occasion on which she is reported as screaming hysterically was on a trip across the Alps on a donkey – she was terrified of falling off the mountain to her death. Her travelling companions found her outbursts upsetting. What the donkey thought is not recorded.

12.3. A search of *The Complete Works of George Eliot* on Google Books reveals that the word 'scream' occurs fifteen times and 'screaming' sixteen times. There are also twelve occurrences of 'screamed' and seven of 'screams'. This seems quite reasonable over seven novels, five shorter stories, quite a lot of poetry (which no one now reads), a couple of translations and some non-fiction.

12.3.1. Most of the screamers are women and girls, but men also scream, as do geese, guinea fowl, water fowl and violins.

12.3.2. The humans' reasons for screaming range from seeing their child covered in mud, finding their gold stolen, a runaway monkey, revealed secrets, discovering a dead body, thinking their husband has died, and with rage while dancing.

12.4. When George Lewes died, Marian broke down, screaming.

12.4.1. I hope that, in similar circumstances, I too would be courageous enough to let go.

13. On biography

13.1. In a review of Thomas Carlyle's biography of his friend, writer John Sterling, George Eliot sets out her ideal biography: 'instead of the dreary three- or five-volumed compilations of letter, and diary, and detail, little to the purpose ... we could have a real "life", setting forth briefly and vividly the man's inward and outward struggles, aims, and achievements, so as to make clear the meaning which his experience has for his fellows'.

13.1.1. As to meaning, I wouldn't dare hazard a guess; but, then again, George Eliot was not a man.

Navigating by the stars

All through the hot day there are loud noises:
a shot, and the birds fly up
as if levitated away from the vines
and, like ink dropped in water
they wheel their dark way
towards the next vineyard

I slept my way into silence
through the afternoon, after days
of too many words and not enough words
to make the map she needs
to find her way from here
I wake, too late, with a headache
and she, in the garden, wakes up shivering

She's always waiting for the stars to be in alignment
and tonight, just after sunset, two planets
will line up just above the horizon
but we miss them
We're too late back from dinner, but
out here in the countryside, when we flick off the light switch
we turn on the stars:
the gentle sprinkling I thought I knew
is nothing to this – someone has taken a titanic brush
and splattered the Milky Way
in a thick band across the crown of the sky

Determined to prove she isn't lost, she starts pointing them out
'See that bright one there? That's a planet

and that one over there, that's a planet too'
They are the brightest things in the sky
and even I know Mars by its reddish glow
She tells me that the stars keep dancing, shaking
disappearing and reappearing
And it's true, those stars, they keep
buzzing around like fireflies
but the planets hold your gaze

She shows me the dark spot next to the Southern Cross
where there are no stars in the midst of stars
It isn't an absence, she says, there is something blocking them
something between them and us
It's not, as I suggest, a black hole
but it *is* something dark, something that doesn't reflect light
'In Botswana', she says, 'they call that gap the Giraffe
That patch is his head, and then there's his neck
and I don't think we can see the rest, not from here
We've named the constellations, they
name the spaces between'

There are so many stories up there, if you know
where to look, how to read them
but I don't
I know Orion, with his pot, but only barely
and then my own Castor and Pollux
I don't believe that our fate is written in the heavens
that the hour of our births, or, in my case, extraction
makes us and yet
I am a split-sided creature
a twin in one, unzipped

'Oh look! Another shooting star'
She has seen five, and I have still not seen any
I try to take in the whole sky at once, to notice
any leaping, to miss nothing
How hard it must be to be God; there is always
something at the corner of your eye
a star disappearing and reappearing
and as your eyes move you imagine
a flash, a splash, but no, but oh!
'I think I saw one!'
'Was it a straight line?'
Yes, a straight streak, a quick burn
a short glory; not a portent
but a reward

The air has dropped to chill
We stay out too late, the dew fallen around us
and talk of the absence, not the one in the sky
but the other, the one she isn't sure she wants to fill
isn't sure it needs filling
or perhaps it's already filled with dark matter
How can you tell if you don't know
whether stars are even on the other side?

The next morning I am grateful for the sun
How strange that it's a star, and yet its light is nothing
like the coolness of the others, millions of miles away
There's a crack, and the birds fly up, again
and away, again, and I half remember
some myth, some story
about a cloud, a cloud that wasn't really a cloud
but a flock of black birds
which flew over and blocked out the sun

The happiness of Mary Shelley
A poem for three voices

Mary

I was no stranger to happiness. I knew it as I once knew every bump on the smoothness of my lover's skin.

I was born under a lucky star, storms and portents heralded my birth. I sprang, fully formed, from the union of two matchless minds. A child of love and light: how could I be anything but filled with promise?

Victor

I have known happiness in such abundance that I could have drowned in it, and God will forgive me when I say that I wish I *had* when I was an innocent child whose eyes did not yet look towards the stars.

Monster

Have I known happiness?
Is it like the burning of ice inside my mouth
as I convoyed across the marzipan continent
the only wedding cake I will ever have?

I think I knew happiness, or something like it
in the moments when I looked back
and saw his dark shape
emerge at my vanishing point
and in the early morning

when I left clues and riddles –
little love letters to my god

Mary

I have known happiness. I knew it in the deluded moments when I thought that I could be accepted as I am. I knew it when I believed my father would lay aside convention, value my conviction. When I believed my father would still love me.

Victor

The spark of knowledge is the phantom, the shadow of happiness.

Knowledge, I believed, was the power of my life force. Without knowledge I would be deadened, but it is better to be dead than to be damned.

Monster

I knew happiness

I knew it in the deluded moments
when I thought I could be
accepted as I am
When I believed
someone could see past my face
value my good acts, my heart

When I believed
my father could love me

Mary

Mary Wollstonecraft Godwin. My very name mocks me: the names of my much-loved, never-known mother; my father who taught me everything but would not be taught by me.

Mary Wollstonecraft Shelley. My name linked forever with his.

Victor

Victor Frankenstein. My very name mocks me: Victor of the stone of the Franks – my great Genovese family, a boulder around my neck.

I am no victor. I am defeated.

Monster

I am the child
who died so soon
after leaving the womb
that I was never named
never mentioned
by the parents who
have no love left
in their hardened hearts

Mary

If you remain childless you do not have to face the horror of the small life force snuffed away, watch the electricity and animation slip from their limbs. Is it better to have loved and tried and lost and failed? Or is a child a monster, rent from your womb to bring misery?

Victor

I am left only half a man. The creature, my doppelgänger, took my reason, but I know he has no heart for I feel it here, still beating in my chest – my ribcage holding it from cracking.

Monster

If I were happy
I would be good

and if I were good
I would be happy
If I were loved
I would be happy

if I were not hated
I would be good

How to live through this

We will make sure we get a good night's sleep. We will eat a decent breakfast, probably involving eggs and bacon. We will make sure we drink enough water. We will go for a walk, preferably in the sunshine. We will gently inhale lungsful of air. We will try to not gulp in the lungsful of air. We will go to the sea. We will watch the waves. We will phone our mothers. We will phone our fathers. We will phone our friends. We will sit on the couch with our friends. We will hold hands with our friends while sitting on the couch. We will cry on the couch with our friends. We will watch movies without tension – comedies or concert movies – on the couch with our friends while holding hands and crying. We will think about running away and hiding. We will think about fighting, both metaphorically and actually. We will consider bricks. We will buy a sturdy padlock. We will lock the gate with the sturdy padlock, even though the gate isn't really high enough. We will lock our doors. We will screen our calls. We will unlist our phone numbers. We will wait. We will make appointments with our doctors. We will make sure to eat our vegetables. We will read comforting books before bedtime. We will make sure our sheets are clean. We will make sure our room is aired. We will make plans. We will talk around it and talk through it and talk it out. We will try to be grateful. We will be grateful. We will make sure we get a good night's sleep.

Forks

There are forks that I like to use, and forks that I do not like to use. Of the latter, we have several in our cutlery drawer. 'Is this fork OK for you?' S asks quizzically, as he fishes one out. 'No', I say. 'Not that one.' He tries another. The forks I do not like but which are in our possession are of two kinds. The first are like ordinary forks, but thinner. Anaemic. Flimsy. Like forks that have not eaten a hearty meal or seen the sunshine or gone for a walk for quite some time, if ever in their lives. The second kind of bad fork is slightly too short in the handle, which widens at a sharp angle towards its end, and which I find causes mild discomfort on my fingers. You might quite reasonably ask me why ever I don't get rid of the forks I don't like and refuse to use. I do have an answer though, which is that if we got rid of them – threw them out or gave them away – we wouldn't have enough forks. Well, you might reply, then why don't you buy new forks, of a kind you like? Ah, now you're getting to the big questions that drive to the heart of my inadequacies. Questions for which I have no justifiable answers.

Four stories about kindness

I had lunch with Y today, and she told me over gnocchi (me) and meatballs (her), about how she joined up with another dating website. She quickly filled in the online forms, all the ones about herself and her interests, until she came to one where she had to choose the five attributes she thought were the most important in a person. She looked at them for a while, and then grabbed a piece of paper and wrote out the thirty possible attributes in a list. She read the list. She put it down and went to bed. The next morning when she woke up she read the list again. She found her scissors and snipped around each word. She laid each rectangle on the table, arranged them in a possible order, shuffled them around, and then arranged them again. She went to work. When she came back in the evening they were still there, glowing slightly in the twilight. She sat down in front of them and made some minor adjustments. She discovered, somewhat to her surprise, that kindness is the most important thing to her. She went back to the web page and finished her application. Very soon she was registered and had been matched with ten men in her area. Soon after she had thirty-five messages. The next morning she had forty more. She deleted the messages and deleted her profile. Then she wrote five words on a piece of paper and pinned it to her wall.

*

I phone A, whose father is dying. Whether fast or slow, no one really knows, and no one wants to say it, but we all know this will probably be his last Christmas. She was, at this very moment, she tells me, writing in our Christmas card. She tells me that she's been thinking a lot about kindness. About people who are kind even when it's inconvenient, even when it hurts. I tell her she is a kind person. 'There are times', she says, 'when I could have chosen to be kind, but I didn't. Wasn't. I've said things. Done things. I don't want to do that – I don't want to make people feel small.' I think of my own list, my own regrets. It's weeks later before we get our Christmas card. 'What's this word here?' asks S, as he reads it. 'Before "lights".' '"Kind",' I say. 'The word is "kind".'

*

J is a scientific sort of person, and she wants to understand relationships, so she does what any good scientist would do and keeps a notebook in which she records her observations. She watches. And listens. And then she writes. She writes about the good ones, and about the bad ones. Her subjects are her friends, her family, her acquaintances and people she meets (or overhears) while travelling. None of them have given ethics approval. (She hasn't asked.) She considers the characteristics of each relationship, both good and bad, and in-between. It is almost halfway through New Year's Day and we are still eating breakfast. While her study is not yet finished, and so all results are of course provisional, she tells us one thing is clear to her already: that the characteristic shared by the best relationships is kindness.

*

I am talking to C in the back yard at the party and I tell him that the theme of the moment is kindness. He tells me that while, yes, he thinks kindness is important, he thinks he is sometimes (for which I read 'often') too kind. He puts up with things, he says, that he should not. He lets people have their way. He doesn't want to hurt their feelings, but he doesn't want to be a doormat anymore. I'm not always the quickest thinker, but I know there is something wrong here; I think I know that there is a difference between kindness and niceness, kindness and martyrdom. I am sure that being kind doesn't mean giving in, going along with things you don't like, denying yourself. I'm sure that being kind doesn't mean you can't give the hard word, when needed, doesn't mean condoning bad behaviour. I try to explain this to C, who *is* kind, and also *is* a doormat sometimes, but I'm not sure he understands what I'm saying. I'm not sure if he heard me. Probably because we are both too busy giving each other advice.

How to live

Memory loves company. He is sitting beside me on the couch and if we turned and looked out the window we would see the tidal part of the harbour that we do not know, but instead we are facing the interior. Because I am telling him his story. This is how we lived. A story is a collection of fragments. A collection of fragments is not a story. Every definition of poetry we can come up with is riddled with flaws. *Where do we begin? Begin with the heart.* Julian of Norwich
It was around this time that I rediscovered my love of swimming, and of dancing, and perhaps they are the same thing? I wanted to be the cat who had swallowed the sun. I wanted to feel the space between melting. I wanted both, and. The gap between is the space for metaphor.

Testing the tender. What have we without fingertips? Let me give it to you slant. There's not much I can't find a shade of grey in. I have been told that men with wives live longer; is it because they are happier, or because they go to the doctor? It was while reading a poem by P that I first discovered the word 'apophenia', a word I had been looking for my whole life. *It's not we who speak language, it's language* Martin Heidegger
that speaks us. I think it's necessary to have subtext. N says yes, but no, not subtext, but metatext. In any case, we both agree surfaces are not enough.

While the doctor is talking, when he says those words, I wait for the floor to fall away from my feet; but it doesn't. A cancer, a can't sir; a question, an answer. He's speaking a language I've never heard, so he writes it down. A line of letters, a shape, a pattern. Metaphor is taking two things and saying they are the same. Metaphor is taking two things and saying there is something that connects them, something akin in them, and yet they are still different. Metaphor is two things shining a light on each other. Placing one thing beside another thing changes them both.

Everything is sweeter: the sun on the waves more sparkling; this afternoon, precious. I don't want to let go of your hand. You insist this bad movie is the one and so we mock our way through it. But it still moves me. At the beginning, darkness is always separated from the light. There are advantages to coming from a stoic family. We have said it so often that we've forgotten it's a metaphor. It wasn't so much a lump as a hardness. When people asked, we said no, we didn't want to escape to the south of France, though perhaps that was because we hadn't been there yet. But we loved our life, we loved our lives. She is trying to live in the moment but says it's hard to stop thinking about the ways each moment could be improved, by, for example, a better seat, or more walnuts. I have never fished, but I imagine it must feel something like this – throwing something out, waiting for it to catch.

It is strange to feel one's own life turn into a cliché. We think we learn from history, but we never do. I always think of memory as a video recording, but it's more like series of bullet points and we construct the rest. This leads, inevitably, to falsity. It isn't enough to remember the ideas – if I have lost the exact words, I have lost the thought. I haven't written *this* poem yet, so I don't know how. I need to learn. Am I a metaphor for something else, or is something else a metaphor for me? I don't want to live an ordinary life, but I know it won't help me when I'm dead. I have long struggled against the tyranny of the line break. Am I afraid that if I let the words leak out, they'll mix with oxygen and become prose?

I can't pinpoint the moment I realised there was no point in having these conversations. There is always a choice, but it is always limited. *Life can only be understood backwards but must be lived forwards.* Is happiness a good mood, or a good life? Essay: to try or attempt. Assay: testing a metal or ore. The doubleness, the splitness, the tension between wasting time and enjoying time, between wanting and getting what you want. I have always felt like a late starter. It was the sun on my red, she said. 'You move like you're moving through water.' *I have already at times been a boy and a girl and a bush / and a bird and mute fish in the salty waves.* The one and the many. We are supposed to know that we are nothing but a body, but who can believe that?

Søren Kierkegaard

Empedocles

What causes it? What is the likelihood of it recurring? What would the surgery involve? What would chemo involve? Would he lose his hair? What are the time frames? When did you first begin dancing, and why? When did you first begin writing, and why? Is there a crossover in the creative process; does one inform the other? How do you know if an idea will be a dance or writing? It is a comfort that I never know how, but manage it anyway.

Apophenia was invented to describe the way people seek patterns and meaning in random information, such as seeing faces in inanimate objects or patterns in gambling numbers. Originally it specifically referred to the extreme pattern recognition that can accompany psychosis. 'I am not a number.' You can say that as often as you like, but once you're in the system, you're barely a human being. I wouldn't die for a tree or a rose garden, but it would be nice just the same. From the blood they take they can measure how much your body has already turned against you and how much of a man you are. Because I fell in love with you, I did not need to be so courageous. Looking for healing, we always come back to moving water, oceans and waves, crashing and calming. 'We're going to pull it out by the roots', says the doctor. I'm waiting for the appointment to start but it's already over, our questions an inconvenience he was willing to tolerate for only a short time. It's not going to kill you, so it's no big deal. In the evening we drink tea together, alone. I have a whole pot to myself but barely sip. I am trying to be a lioness. My paws are shaking.

As hungers grow, so too frustrations. I cannot bear that much raw honesty, even to myself, even from myself. *There is much to be learned from wanting something both ways.* The impossibility of keeping hold is part of the attraction. Sometimes love is a decision. Is poetry just writing with white space? And then you hear murmuring through the walls, or floor, that might be your own blood in your own veins, it might be one side of a conversation, but which side you can't quite make out. Sooner or later the honest memoirist is forced to face it: the fallibility of memory. In my memory, we held hands the whole time, smiling in the face of it. Sometimes memory is better, sometimes worse. The angles are sharper. Trying to not cry and then trying to cry, but this is a desert and we are dry cactus. 1 a.m. is a bad time for a misunderstanding. 'I've realised I've been too passive in my life', he says.

What is walking but falling and catching, falling and catching? Finity is the tragedy of our lives. I'm not one for answers, though I do love giving advice – I dole it out like ten-cent mixtures, with the same gently fizzing chalky discs and a couple of wine gums. It is a mistake to think that others are like ourselves, but mapping is a hard urge to resist. The thing that makes the poem is how you read it. I'm thinking about resonance. I'm thinking about vision coming

Maggie Nelson

William James — into focus. *Consciousness, then, does not appear to itself chopped up in bits.* Poetry is seen, by default, as an autobiographical form by people who have not heard of the biographical fallacy, and by those who have but do not believe it.

You said, then I said, then you said, then I didn't say, and you didn't say and you said, and I said and then it was too late to take it back. Trying to relax in this house of hard surfaces, hard edges, brittle. I used to be afraid of breathing too loudly. Breathing is an expansive gesture. The three-part inhale: the breath of joy. Some days the feelings are too big for me to think away. I look for it every time I take this road, the words yarn-bombed on the wire fence: 'You are doing OK.' Thank you, I say, I needed that. A problem shared is a problem halved, except when it's a problem doubled. Empathy is overrated. Empathy is underrated. Is it just the putting on of another's pain like a pair of trousers? Does it necessarily involve action, and if so, what kind?

I do not mean to be uneasy. You can't catch cancer from grief the same as you can't catch a cold from being cold, and yet we know they are connected. A kind of antimatter, so heavy it can't be borne. Her own mother knitted herself only five more years after her husband died. I am thinking about our need to split ourselves – to be able to look at ourselves critically and take responsibility, while also being kind. Being kind isn't as easy as it sounds.

The one and the many, the many and the multiple. Metaxu: a wall that separates two prisoners can be used to tap messages. *Every separation is a link.* In this too much sadness is it my obligation to enjoy this patch of spring sunlight and rejoice?

Simone Weil

Disaster revealed to me that much of what we've been taught about human nature is not true. I am tired of being a functional human being. I had just stepped on when I lost the knack of balance and nearly fell. I have since learned to make sure there is someone just ahead of me – a stranger will do, a friend better. I am afraid to become the married man in 'A Married Man's Story'. The people you expect to be there for you are not always the ones who are. If you expected the unexpected it would be expected. One of the things I have always loved about him is the way he is unpredictably unpredictable. This teapot, for example, is a real object, but it's also a symbol of our relationship. You don't just learn to read one time, but over and over again.

Rebecca Solnit

We are preparing to go on a long journey, or, in two days' time we will enter a biodome, go into hibernation, fall into a wormhole; there is so much to do, but the moment hangs in the air, suspended animation. Perhaps we will be frozen for 500 years, find ourselves, unblinking, in a time we cannot recognise, where people don't even use words anymore, communicating instead with movement, scent and intuition. Or maybe you are going to the hospital and I am waiting for you, and then you'll come home, and we'll wait together.

Igor Stravinsky

Sometimes when I read, I have to try to not let jealousy get in the way. I once wrote a poem under the influence of T. S. Eliot, in the way one is under the influence of alcohol after a glass and a half of wine; I would read a little of *The Waste Land* and then turn to my poem, which bore no resemblance and yet I hoped a rhythm, a heartbeat, may have passed over. Table tapping. I am amazed at how the same words can be so different. *I wonder if memory is true, and I know that it cannot be, but that one lives by memory nonetheless and not by truth.*

Jacques Lacan

It is possible that I am looking for answers, but I'm not looking for *the* answer. Why should strength come from certainty? *The reason we go to poetry is not for wisdom, but for the dismantling of wisdom.* B says he was taught patience by the Church of England. I had planned to take *Middlemarch*, a thick green world to climb into during the waiting, a protest against the dull carpet, but in the rush to leave Dorothea, Ladislaw, Fred Vincy and the rest got left behind on the table, and so the best I could find was *Oprah* magazine. By the end of the waiting we had become scratchy children, trapped in the room with the television. We came to blows.

T asks a question on Facebook: 'What are the things that make you happy?' 'Good friends.' 'Good food.' 'Wine and chocolate and a warm bed.' 'Music.' 'Creating art.' 'Reading, learning, travelling to cool places.' 'My children.' 'Loving and being loved.' 'You.' Art is supposed to ask questions, not give answers; but perhaps some tentative suggestions are permissible? 1) Time, and the ability to enjoy the time; 2) space, and the ability to enjoy the space; 3) money, with a) the ability to enjoy it, and b) being able to obtain it with little wastage of time and space.

And now we wait. It seems impossible that there could be anything bad inside of you. A scar in the hip-fold, invisible now, just another line on the skin. *You are the mountain and the valley.* S says, 'Time is your friend as well as your enemy. God knows, you don't want to live in some of your moments forever.' We made a lot of time for nostalgia: Kirk, Spock, Bones – the whole brain – a past future more advanced than the present, more hopeful. Sometimes I read something and forget every line as if instead I had read a book in which all the pages were blank. Time, it must be said, is a constant shock.

Hildegard von Bingen

An essay is a search, an enquiry. An essay is a question. *[A]ll completeness is falsehood.* I had an idea that a good metaphor for what I am trying to do was enamelling, thinking it involved building up many thin layers of lacquer to create a jewel-like depth, but when I checked I discovered enamelling is the fusion of glass with

Theodor Adorno

metal through the application of intense heat. Perhaps the metaphor stands. Even more than libraries, hospitals are the only places that everyone goes. They are made up of waiting rooms, though this one is just a brief widening of the corridor, a cupboard with no door. Should I be bothered if, as I fear, poetry is a form of popular philosophy, of self-help? Don't we need all the help we can get?

N says she thinks it's something to do with how poetry treats time. I am forever putting my friends in. They are my synecdoche, my to-hand examples. I am not unaware of the smallness of my sample. *In philosophy one thinks only metaphorically.* S says he prefers someone to be a dick in public but kind to their friends and family over someone who is kind in public but a dick to their friends and family. I can tell we are both holding men in our minds. I say I hate hypocrisy above all things, and immediately start thinking of things I hate more.

Louis Althusser

I like the way she tap, tap, taps your vein, as if checking it's real, like it's jelly to wobble, and how she shows you where to put your fingertip, so you can feel it rushing in under your skin. 'You might feel lightheaded and nauseous, you might taste something or smell something, you might feel like you've wet your pants, but you haven't; these are all normal side effects.' Is metaphor a war or a cooperation? Is metaphor a conflict or a love affair? What is the opposite of metaphor?

I'm afraid to start until I'm in the middle, and then I'm afraid to end. The beautiful, terrifying moments when you feel you are on the edge of it all coming together. *In the greatest art, one is always aware of the things that cannot be said.* When I tell A that it's no use regretting the past because you can't change it but you can change the future, she tells me to shut up. But by the next week she has taken a leap. Sometimes the rumour of death jolts you to life. It is probably because I had just walked past the School of Philosophy that I misread the sign on the drain-unblocking truck as 'Brain Unlocking'. Excuse me, I wish to make an appointment.

Susan Sontag

What is the difference between not doing the wrong thing, and doing the right thing? V said that the biggest thing she learned is to do all those things you want to do; and then she told me about the woman who lived in her apartment building who really wanted a dog, who would imagine taking the dog for walks and runs, who lamented that she wasn't allowed to have a dog in the apartment, but who never moved. *There's only one story, the story of your life.* It's better to run towards something rather than away from something. A cliché is just something that has been said too many times.

Helen Keller

All going well, I'm already about halfway through my life, and still almost everything to do. 'I'm just the same as I was', she says, 'only sadder.' I admit that I am happier, but claim it was hard won – feeling that being sadder might be cooler, even though, having been sadder, I know it is not. I don't want a quiet life, but I do want a lot of quiet. I have found that most people will shrink back from intensity; a good life may be a moderate one, but I am not yet ready to accept it. *Only the dead fail to reach out with both hands.* When M died, K talked about the way he had deliberately created those perfect spontaneous moments, like running through Venice in the light rain.

<small>Christine de Pisan</small>

She is the warmest person we have ever met in the hospital. She is not even wearing a disguise. She tells us your story: 'There was this, and so we tested for that, and we found this and so we did that, and then . . .' and by the punchline we both fear she is trying to tell us you have something worse, but instead she says the closest thing they could ever say to: 'You are cured.' I want to hug her, but I don't think that's allowed. When your unit is a sentence; when your life is months, days, hours. The best books are the ones you read slowly because you never want them to end. *If we knew the value of suffering, we would ask for it.* 'Though I have learned a lot from my mother, mainly about how not to live, she did teach me that it isn't the first thought that counts, but the second – "Think again", she's always saying to me, "think again".'

<small>Brother André</small>

Top five regrets of the dying, as recorded by a palliative care nurse: 1) I wish I'd had the courage to live a life true to myself, not the life others expected of me. 2) I wish I hadn't worked so hard. 3) I wish I'd had the courage to express my feelings. 4) I wish I'd stayed in touch with my friends. 5) I wish that I had let myself be happier. 'I understand the Tooth Fairy', he says, 'something in return for what you've lost.' Fifty cents doesn't cut it anymore, so we're on our way to Reinga; but we're coming back.

Reaping what we sow: how simple, how painful. But whatever you sow, there will always be weeds. Forgive me, I do not mean to be so negative. She has started writing every night a list of three good things from her day; some days they make her feel good and grateful, other days she thinks: 'Is that really all?!' *The act of writing is an act of resistance against the mortal condition – not against mortality, but the mortal condition.* I had been trying to write this poem for many years before I read Lyn Hejinian's *My Life* and learned how to, like the piece of a puzzle had slotted in – the last of the top edge of sky.

Robert Dessaix

The beginning is always today. We have left the unfamiliar harbour and head back towards the top. It has been seven years. I know it is a magical number, but can't remember why. The light has become too dull to read our books. We are out of range, we are outside of time. The point of metaphor is not even so much getting people to think of the comparison of A and B, but of seeing A in a new way. What's the point of having deep roots if you're not growing? You say: 'I want to be a big tree.'

Mary Wollstonecraft

Simone de Beauvoir

There is something about poetry that tells us to slow down, to pay attention, look for meaning – the same way the gravel road told you to take your time, breathe more deeply. But they've replaced the gravel with prose, poetry with asphalt, and before we know it we are there, wondering if instead we should have walked up the beach with the other spirits. *I am incapable of conceiving infinity, and yet I do not accept finity.* How can something that has been said so many times still have any meaning? And yet, I love you. This is the way we reclaim each other. Around the lighthouse has also changed, they've built walls to stop us from sitting on the grassy slope as we watch the meeting of two oceans, which is an actual thing and not only a metaphor. Apophenia – I take the three things we see: the signposts pointing to the ends of the earth, the aeroplane overhead and the swallow I recognise only by its forked tail, and decide this is a sign.

Notes

The sources of most of the quotations used in the poems are acknowledged, however inadequately, within the text. Additionally, in 'Ban Zhao' the extracts in quotation marks are from Ban Zhao's treatise *Lessons for Women* and the definitions of 'yin', 'yang' and 'yin-yang' are adapted from the *Oxford English Dictionary* by way of the *Wikipedia* entry on 'Yin and Yang'.

The Sisi Museum, featured in 'I knew we were really supposed to take the audio guides' is a museum in the Hofburg palace in Vienna dedicated to Empress Elisabeth (1837–1898), affectionately known as Sisi, the last empress of Austria.

I'm grateful to the many sources I used when researching 'George Eliot: a life'; the main ones I returned to again and again were *George Eliot: A Life* by Rosemary Ashton, *George Eliot: The Last Victorian* by Kathryn Hughes, and *The Road to Middlemarch: My Life With George Eliot* by Rebecca Mead. This year, 2019, is the 200th anniversary of George Eliot/Mary Anne Evans's birth, which feels auspicious.

'Navigating by the stars' says that we name the constellations, while the people of Botswana name the spaces between. I've since learned (from *Te Ara – the Encyclopedia of New Zealand*) that in English the dark patch next to the Southern Cross is called 'the Coal Sack', which is not quite as delightful as 'the Giraffe'.

Readers of Maggie Nelson's wonderful book *The Argonauts* will recognise the neat referencing system which I borrowed for use in 'How to live'.

Acknowledgements

Some of these poems or extracts from these poems have previously been published in *Turbine | Kapohau, Trout, Landfall, Rabbit, NZ Poetry Shelf, Blackmail Press* (the Rebel Issue), *Eye to the Telescope, Dominion Post* and the *Vic Books Poetry Day Zine 2016*.

Grateful acknowledgements to Creative New Zealand for the grant I received to assist with the writing of this book. The focused time it made possible allowed me to go much deeper, and read and think and write much more than I could have otherwise.

Enormous thanks also to my poetry peeps, who have been unfailingly supportive of me and this book, most especially Anna Jackson and Angelina Sbroma (I mainly finished it so you two could read it), Vana Manasiadis and many others; and also, always, Sean Molloy. Thank you to Poetry Club for your feedback on drafts of some of these poems. Thank you to my friends, my synecdoche, my to-hand examples, for putting up with me for putting you in – I hope I haven't misrepresented you too much. Thank you to the attendees of Truth or Beauty: Poetry and Biography (2014), and Poetry and the Essay: Form and Fragmentation (2019) – our collective thinking at those conferences fed into many of these poems. Thank you to Sarah Jane Barnett for careful copyediting, and especially checking all those names. Thanks to Carolyn Lewis for designing such a beautiful book for my words to live in. And thank you to the team at Auckland University Press – Sam, Katharina, Andy and Sophia – for shepherding this book into the world.

First published 2019
Auckland University Press
University of Auckland
Private Bag 92019
Auckland 1142
New Zealand
www.press.auckland.ac.nz

© Helen Rickerby, 2019

ISBN 978 1 86940 905 0

A catalogue record for this book is available from the National Library of New Zealand

This book is copyright. Apart from fair dealing for the purpose of private study, research, criticism or review, as permitted under the Copyright Act, no part may be reproduced by any process without prior permission of the publisher. The moral rights of the author have been asserted.

Design by Carolyn Lewis

Printed in Singapore by Markono Print Media Pte Ltd